CATS SET VI

HAVANA BROWN CATS

Jill C. Wheeler
ABDO Publishing Company

Published by ABDO Publishing Company, PO Box 398166, Minneapolis, MN 55439.
Copyright © 2012 by Abdo Consulting Group, Inc. International copyrights reserved
in all countries. No part of this book may be reproduced in any form without written
permission from the publisher. The Checkerboard Library™ is a trademark and logo of
ABDO Publishing Company.

Printed in the United States of America, North Mankato, Minnesota.
102011
012012

 PRINTED ON RECYCLED PAPER

Cover Photo: Photo by Helmi Flick
Interior Photos: Alamy p. 19; Animals Animals p. 16; Photos by Helmi Flick pp. 5, 7, 9,
    10, 11, 13, 15, 17, 21

Editors: Megan M. Gunderson, BreAnn Rumsch
Art Direction: Neil Klinepier

Library of Congress Cataloging-in-Publication Data

Wheeler, Jill C., 1964-
  Havana brown cats / Jill C. Wheeler.
      p. cm. -- (Cats)
  Includes index.
  ISBN 978-1-61783-241-3
  1. Havana brown cat--Juvenile literature. I. Title.
  SF449.H53W44 2012
  636.83--dc23
                        2011026460

CONTENTS

Lions, Tigers, and Cats

Most pet cats don't look much like the lions we see in the zoo. Yet pet cats and lions are both members of the family **Felidae**. Whether pet cats or wild lions, members of this family are all outstanding hunters!

The **domestic** cat is one of 37 species in this family. Within that species, there are more than 40 different **breeds**.

These breeds developed when humans first began domesticating cats more than 3,500 years ago. Humans used cats to control the **rodents** that threatened their stored grain. This created a new partnership. The cats took care of the **rodents**, and the humans took care of the cats.

Over time, humans began **breeding** particular cats to encourage certain qualities and looks. In the case of Havana brown cats, humans wanted a cat the color of chocolate. By creating these beautiful brown cats, they also created a treasured pet.

Havana browns are one of the rarest cat breeds.

HAVANA BROWN CATS

Today's Havana brown cat is a **hybrid breed**. This means humans created it on purpose. They combined different breeds to create the solid brown, green-eyed cats we now know as Havana browns.

Hundreds of years ago, a naturally all-brown cat existed in Siam, which is now Thailand. In the late 1800s, travelers brought these brown cats to Great Britain. These unusual cats were popular for a while. But in the 1920s, they disappeared from cat shows.

In the 1950s, five English breeders wanted to bring back green-eyed, solid brown cats. So,

they **bred domestic** shorthair cats, Siamese cats, and Russian blue cats to create the perfect combination.

A Havana brown cat first came to the United States in the mid-1950s. The breed was accepted for registration in the **Cat Fanciers' Association (CFA)** in 1959.

Some people think the name Havana brown comes from the color of the Havana rabbit.

QUALITIES

Havana browns are **unique** in how they learn about their surroundings. Most cats rely on their sense of smell. But graceful Havana brown cats also use their paws. They are more likely than other **breeds** to explore things by touching and feeling them.

This breed is intelligent and affectionate. They crave attention and will often reach out and touch their humans or raise a paw in greeting. They are happy to cuddle up with their owners or with other cats. In fact, they are happiest when they can be involved in everything their owners do.

Havana browns speak in quiet, gentle voices. These smart cats tend to attach themselves to just one owner for life. This may make them seem shy, but many are outgoing.

With enough attention, Havana brown cats do very well in single-owner homes. These playful pets can also get along with other pets, including dogs.

Havana browns are not as active as some other breeds. But these alert felines are not couch potatoes!

COAT AND COLOR

Havana browns are the only breed with a specific whisker color required for show cats.

Havana browns are known for their rich, glossy coats. They are solid chocolate brown, reddish-brown, or mahogany in color. Even their whiskers are brown to match! The **CFA** prefers warm brown tones over black-brown shades.

The Havana brown's coat features short to medium-length fur. So,

Havana browns are nicknamed "brownies."

this **breed** doesn't **shed** much. Their coats are
close-lying, thick, and very smooth. They feel silky
to the touch.

Havana browns are also known for their vivid
green eyes! They have rosy pink paw pads and
rosy-toned brown noses. This contrasts beautifully
with their lovely dark coats.

SIZE

Many people are surprised when they pick up Havana brown cats. These elegant cats look as though they would be lightweight. Yet their toned, muscular build makes them feel surprisingly heavy!

Havana browns are medium-sized cats. Adults weigh an average of six to ten pounds (2.5 to 4.5 kg). Females are slightly smaller than males. Their legs are slimmer than the male's well-muscled legs. The Havana brown's legs feature small paws. The tail tapers to a point.

The Havana brown's head has a **unique** shape. It is longer than it is wide. These cats have large, wide-set ears that tilt forward. They make the cats look alert and expressive. The Havana's green eyes are oval, medium sized, and set wide apart.

The tail is usually carried high above the back or curled forward.

CARE

Havana brown cats tend to be very healthy. Yet like all cats, they will need to visit a veterinarian at least once a year. The veterinarian will provide **vaccines** for kittens and adults. It also is a good idea to **spay** or **neuter** cats that will not be **bred**.

This breed does best indoors. Owners should supply a scratching post where Havanas can sharpen their claws. Owners should also provide plenty of safe toys. Havana browns enjoy stealing whatever they can pick up in their mouths! Yet these intelligent cats can also learn to play fetch.

Regular grooming will help keep your Havana brown happy and healthy. Brush its coat once or twice a week to keep it glossy. Even smoothing the coat with your hands will help keep it in good condition. Regular nail trimming also is important since these cats use their paws to experience the world.

Annual checkups with a veterinarian will help keep your cat in top condition.

FEEDING

Havana browns require a healthy diet to keep their beautiful mahogany coats in top condition. They have no **unique** nutritional needs. So, any high-quality pet food with plenty of protein will do.

Quality foods can be found in dry, moist, and semimoist varieties. Providing clean, fresh water every day is also vital to your cat's health.

Havana brown owners should take care not to let their cats overeat. These cats will eat their own food and

16

any other pet's food if left out! So, owners should provide only as much food as their cats need at a particular time.

The muscular body of a Havana brown tends not to show weight gain. If you suspect your cat is too heavy, check with your veterinarian. An overweight cat can develop health issues such as **diabetes** and joint problems.

Adult Havana browns are not very interested in people food. But kittens will want to try whatever their owners are having!

KITTENS

Mother Havana browns are **pregnant** for about 65 days. They usually have **litters** of two to four kittens.

Often, Havana brown kittens have light **tabby** markings. These fade over time. The coat usually turns its signature reddish-brown within two years. Other kittens are born with lilac-colored fur and whiskers. This coat is not accepted by the **CFA**.

Kittens may not be available for sale until they are 12 to 16 weeks old. By then, the **breeder** has a good idea of whether the cat is of show quality.

By this time, the kittens also have started receiving their **vaccines**. And, they should know how to use a **litter box**. They should also be used to having a grooming routine and being handled. Their personalities may already be obvious, too!

At birth, the kittens cannot see or hear. These senses begin to function when the kittens are about 10 to 12 days old.

Buying a Kitten

Havana brown cats are rare. If there were a list of endangered cat **breeds**, the Havana brown would be on it! Have you decided this is the right breed for you? It may take a while to find a breeder. And even then, they may place you on a waiting list.

Reputable breeders will want to know about you before selling you a kitten. You may be asked to provide information on your lifestyle and where you live. This way the breeder will know if his or her beloved kittens will be going to a good home.

It is a good idea for you to visit the breeder's location, too. This will let you know if the breeder is dedicated to the health and happiness of his or her cats. It will also help reveal whether this **unique breed**'s personality is a good fit for you.

Havana brown cats are a special breed. With lots of attention and good care, they will be devoted pets for 8 to 13 years.

The Havana brown has been called a natural shoulder sitter. Owners should not be surprised if their cats spend a lot of time riding around on them!

GLOSSARY

breed - a group of animals sharing the same ancestors and appearance. A breeder is a person who raises animals. Raising animals is often called breeding them.

Cat Fanciers' Association (CFA) - a group that sets the standards for judging all breeds of cats.

diabetes - a disease in which the body cannot properly absorb normal amounts of sugar and starch.

domestic - tame, especially relating to animals. To domesticate something is to adapt it to life with humans.

Felidae (FEHL-uh-dee) - the scientific Latin name for the cat family. Members of this family are called felids. They include lions, tigers, leopards, jaguars, cougars, wildcats, lynx, cheetahs, and domestic cats.

hybrid - an offspring of two animals or plants of different races, breeds, varieties, species, or genera.

litter - all of the kittens born at one time to a mother cat.

litter box - a box filled with cat litter, which is similar to sand. Cats use litter boxes to bury their waste.

neuter (NOO-tuhr) - to remove a male animal's reproductive glands.

pregnant - having one or more babies growing within the body.

rodent - any of several related animals that have large front teeth for gnawing. Common rodents include mice, squirrels, and beavers.

shed - to cast off hair, feathers, skin, or other coverings or parts by a natural process.

spay - to remove a female animal's reproductive organs.

tabby - a coat pattern featuring stripes or splotches of a dark color on a lighter background. Individual hairs are banded with light and dark colors.

unique - being the only one of its kind.

vaccine (vak-SEEN) - a shot given to prevent illness or disease.

WEB SITES

To learn more about Havana brown cats, visit ABDO Publishing Company online. Web sites about Havana brown cats are featured on our Book Links page. These links are routinely monitored and updated to provide the most current information available.

www.abdopublishing.com

INDEX